Room to Learn:

WORKING SPACE, LANGUAGE AREAS, AND A PLACE TO PAINT

Joan Dean
Chief Inspector for Primary Schools, Surrey, England

CITATION PRESS   NEW YORK   1974

Acknowledgements

I should like to thank the schools and teachers who
have developed the ideas in this book for their gener-
osity in passing them on to others. I should particularly
like to thank the following schools for allowing me
to use photographs of the ideas they have developed.

Nine Mile Ride School
South Lake Junior School
Crowthorne C. E. School
Springfield Primary School
Brightwell-cum-Sotwell Primary School
St. John's Infant School, Mortimer
Westwood Farm Junior School

Published in the United States by Citation Press,
Library and Trade Division, Scholastic Magazines, Inc.
Editorial Office, 50 West 44th Street, New York, N.Y.
100036

Library of Congress Catalog Card Number: 74-15110
International Standard Book Number: 0-590-09587-0

Contents

WORKING SPACE

Primary education is changing very rapidly. This creates many problems, one of which is that today's approaches to work have to be attempted in buildings and with furniture which was designed for very different teaching methods. Modifications and improvements are taking place all the time, but many teachers are still left with the problem of how to make the best use of existing space and how best to spend any money allocated to them.

The schools of yesterday were planned on the basis of the whole class unit, in which it was intended that children should remain in their desks all the time, with equipment and books distributed and collected by the teacher or by monitors. Learning and teaching were mainly verbal and a class or at least a group worked together. Today we expect children to move about the entire learning area and to collect their own books and materials when they need them.

We have begun to realise that to be effective, verbal education must be based upon first-hand experience; that a child will learn more easily if he is allowed to see and handle materials and make his own deductions; that practical work is an essential element in all learning.

We have recently become more aware of learning differences in children and the need to provide a variety of stimulus and motivation if we are to cater for the differences in the children in our care. This thinking has led to changes in organisation, nearly all of which are designed to make learning a more individual affair, where we attempt to match the work to the needs of the individual child. We try to cater for the differing lengths of time which children need at different tasks and so we often have a variety of activities going on at the same time. This also tends to make for a more efficient use of space, equipment and of teachers' time.

These changes in organisation demand a different use of buildings and equipment than was common in the past. If, for example, it is possible for children to work with little supervision from the teacher, much more of the space in a school can be used. If it is possible for children to paint or use clay at most times of the day, it is possible to reserve a space specifically for this type of activity and to arrange it accordingly. The paint and clay can then be kept away from the parts of a room where clean work goes on and, since there are never forty children painting at once, there is no longer any need to buy forty identical paint brushes. Both space and equipment can thus be used more efficiently.

It is probably true to say that space is our greatest need in schools today. Teachers need to look critically at every square foot of the building, for few schools can afford to have any space out of use for much of the day.

There are a number of places in school buildings which tend to be under-used, which with some minor adaptations might provide further space for work. The plans on page 5 show some of the kinds of areas which are available for use in some schools. The pages following show some of the ways in which such spaces can be adapted for use.

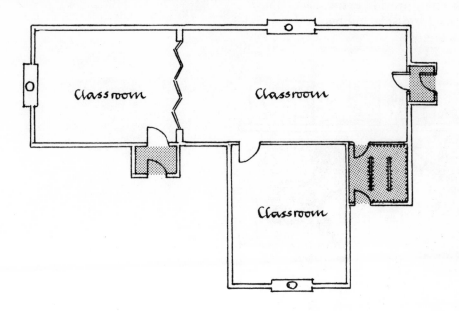

In many really old school buildings there is not a great deal of under-used space, but some have generous cloakrooms and some have porches which might be used.

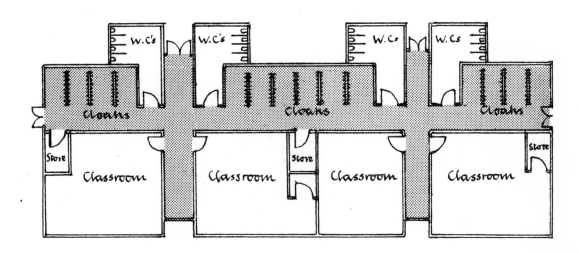

Schools built between the wars and in the nineteen-forties and -fifties usually have a great deal of space in the wrong places. Cloakrooms and corridors are often over generous and there are often more store rooms than are needed. Sometimes there is a stage, which is rarely needed with today's work in drama. All these spaces can be used.

Corridors can often provide extra space. They are a good place for displaying books if narrow-lipped shelves are used.

If a corridor is wide enough to put tables and chairs near the books this may serve as an extra working area for a small group of children.

It may even be possible to provide a length of work top which can be used for work with books or for other activities.

Open shelves in a corridor may provide a place for display, or for storage of shared equipment or materials.

A wide corridor can make an excellent space for a shopping centre, where shopping activities for several classes or groups may be shared.

A corridor work top may provide a useful space for activities like painting or modelling.

A board for painting may be propped against a wall on top of a work bench if the bench has a lip along the front edge to hold it.

An area of pinboard in a corridor can be used for large paintings.

A series of pegs in a bench top will also hold boards for painting and can be removed when the surface is needed for other work.

A secluded corridor can provide space for noisy
activities like woodwork or explorations with
sounds and musical instruments.

Some toys and play materials, like bricks, and
small apparatus may be better used in a corridor.

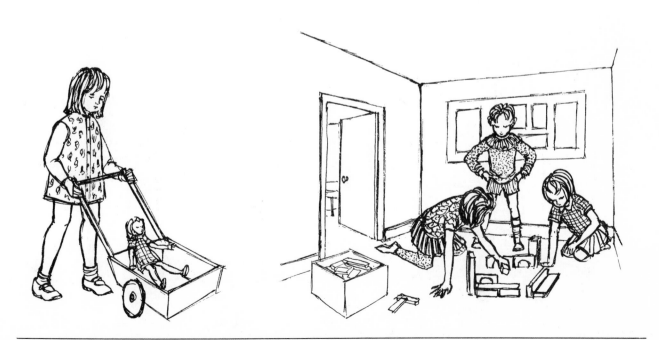

The entrance halls of some schools are larger than they need to be and it is sometimes possible to make use of this space. It may make a good place for a book area, particularly if it can be attractively furnished with some carpet and comfortable chairs.

The entrance hall may also be an excellent place for display: both display of children's work and for stimulus exhibitions of all kinds. It is helpful if there are display surfaces at different levels and somewhere from which fabrics can be hung.

It is often possible to find extra space in a school by using some of the cloakroom space. Cloakrooms sometimes have floors which are suitable for such activities as work with clay.

Cloakrooms with stone or tiled floors may be good places for work with water and sand.

Extra space is sometimes found by re-arranging cloak pegs. There may be more pegs than necessary and some can be removed. Perhaps they are further apart than they need to be.

Sometimes pegs can be moved to a wall which cannot be used for any other purpose, freeing an area for other productive use.

When new washing facilities are being installed it may be possible to have a trough sink instead of a wash basin. This could have a dual use.

A spare cloak bay can be used as a work space or for storage.

Sometimes the end of a cloak rack can be filled in to provide extra display space, or a space where one or two children can work quietly with books.

Sometimes a space above coat racks can be used for display.

Space above cloak racks can also be shelved to provide additional storage.

Additional space may sometimes be made by using a coat trolley, which may be housed in a bay. Coat trolleys can be bought or made with Dexion Speedframe.

Trolleys can be made with pegs for hanging coats.

They can also be made with coat hangers. These take up very little room, but are difficult for the younger children to use.

Storage for a coat trolley can sometimes be made
by removing shelves and doors from a built-in
cupboard.

A store cupboard can also be fitted with a rail
for coat hangers.

Shoe storage can be a problem. A tray for shoes can be incorporated as part of a trolley. This will take wellingtons as well as shoes.

They can hang upside down between two slats. It helps to keep pairs of wellingtons together if children peg them with clothes pegs.

Wellingtons can also be stored on a rack.

A wooden shelf can be useful for storing shoes.
Wire cages may also be used.

A battery of wire cages will provide shoe
storage under a work top, but if too many
children need to use it at once it can cause
congestion.

Surplus shoe cages have many classroom uses.

Many schools find it helpful to think in terms of areas for particular activities. Sometimes these are areas within a classroom and sometimes they are areas shared by two or more classes or a teaching team, and include parts of cloakrooms and corridors.

To some extent this arrangement pre-supposes a situation where a variety of activities goes on at the same time: where some children may be reading or writing, others working with materials and others perhaps working at mathematics or science.

In planning classroom or work-area layout, it is wise to make a basic division between clean and messy work and between quiet and noisy work. When it is possible to use adjoining cloak or corridor space, the noisy and messy activities can be carried on in these areas and the quiet and clean activities can be confined to the classroom, or conversely.

The types of areas provided will vary from school to school, but the following have all been found useful:

A book area and a place for reading and writing
An area for work with materials
A science and mathematics area
A place for environmental studies
A music area
An area or areas for using audio visual equipment
A display area
A home corner
A cooking area
A shopping centre
A place for play with large equipment and toys

It is not usually possible to provide all these areas all the time. It will be necessary to have a permanent reading and writing area and mathematics space, but music areas, cooking areas and others may be devoted to different activities according to current interests and needs. Play areas in infant schools and areas for work with materials will be needed all the time, but may be used for different kinds of work or play at different times. The school of the future will also need good permanent audio-visual areas.

In planning the layout of a classroom or work area, it may be helpful to consider the following questions:

1. What learning activities will take place in this area?
2. What is the maximum number of children likely to be, who will be working at each activity at any given time?
3. What does each activity need in terms of working space—table top, work top or floor?
4. What equipment is needed for each activity?
5. What materials will be needed for each activity?
6. How are pieces of equipment, materials and work in progress to be stored?
7. What individual storage will children need for their personal possessions?
8. What movement about the room will there be?

When all these questions have been considered, we can go on to look at how this kind of provision can be achieved, for even in well-designed new schools it is not possible to provide everything which may be desirable. Teachers will need to improvise in all kinds of ways to create suitable working areas. The following pages look at some of the ways in which this can be done.

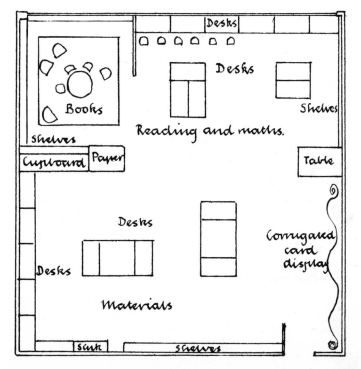

In this classroom there has been an attempt to separate clean and quiet work from messy and noisy work. The part of the room used for work with materials has been dictated by the position of the sink. The twenty dual locker-desks have been used as worktops.

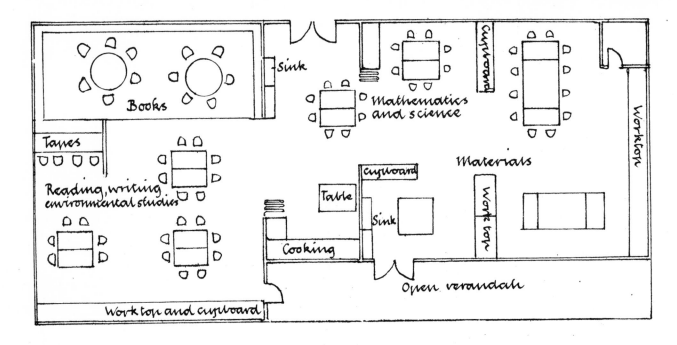

This two-classroom unit was re-organised by the teachers working there on the basis of separating clean and quiet from messy and noisy activities. It was planned for a group of top juniors.

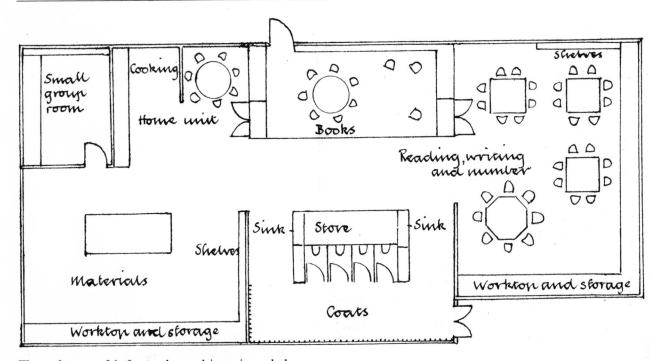

Two classes of infants share this unit and the teachers work together with all the children in the group.

If spaces are to be used for particular activities
room dividers will be needed.

Ideally, we would like purpose-made screens.
This screen is free standing.

Hinged screens can also be useful but tend to be
unstable. A screen can be made from a clothes
horse.

A room divider may be fixed to the back of a
work top or cupboard.

In practice we often have to improvise.
Cupboards make good room dividers, but it is
wise to fix tall cupboards to the floor so that
there is no danger of their tipping over.

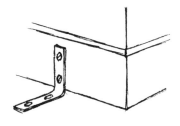

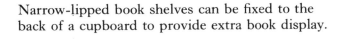

A cupboard back may provide extra display
space.

Narrow-lipped book shelves can be fixed to the
back of a cupboard to provide extra book display.

There are a number of simple ways of making screens and supporting them with home-made stands.

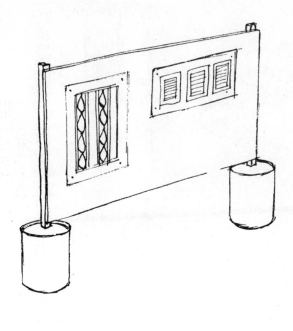
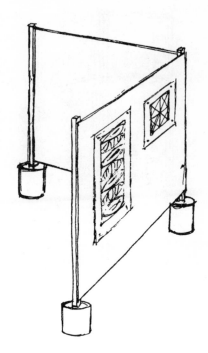

An effective, though not very decorative, support can be made by filling tins with concrete and placing supports in them while the concrete is wet.

These can support screens made of various materials and can be used to make corners and booths. Corrugated card can be wound round two of these supports.

Shelving which can be used from both sides is useful. It can be made easily with Dexion Speedframe.

An old blackboard has been fixed between bookshelves to make a room divider.

Trellis or a board can be fixed between tables to provide divisions of space.

Tables or work tops can be used to divide one
space from another.

Corrugated card can also be used without
supports to make bays and divisions in a room.

In infant and junior work areas where there is little class teaching, space can be increased considerably by not providing a table and chair place for every child.

All children will need working surfaces at some time during the day, but if the programme is flexible they will not all need them at the same time. Some may work at tables or on the floor; others may sit or stand at work tops.

When children come together with their teacher to listen to a story or to discuss something, they can sit on chairs or on the floor. It helps if some carpet is available.

11486

Carpet will also provide a space where children can work on the floor with small equipment or apparatus. It is wise to fix carpet down with a metal strip so that the edges do not get kicked up.

Another way is to use adhesive carpet squares. These have the advantage that they can be laid easily and are firmly fixed in place by the adhesive. The carpeted area can be increased as money becomes available, and worn tiles can easily be replaced.

Yet another way of providing carpet is to collect a number of carpet samples which blend well together and to stick these to a hessian backing or on to a worn carpet with Copydex.

When space is limited it may be worth making hinged work tops attached to the wall which can be used when extra working surface is needed.

These can be hinged downwards or upwards. If they hinge upwards extra display space can be provided on the under side.

Locker desks can be converted for practical work by fitting a lid over a group of them.

Another way of increasing work surface when necessary is to place a board, preferably with a vinyl surface, between two locker desks. It can be fixed to battens on the backs of the desks.

This can be done even more easily by fixing cotton reels to the board so that they fit into the inkwell holes on the desks. This has the disadvantage of a change of surface level, but it is easy to remove and store the board.

Some schools are finding that stools provide easily moved seating which has many uses, and which can be pushed under tables or work tops when not needed.

Stools can be made from old chairs by removing the backs and making cushions for the seats. If the legs are painted and pleasant colours are used for the cushions, these can look quite attractive.

Upholstered stools can be pushed together to make window seats. Long cushions can be used to make bench seats.

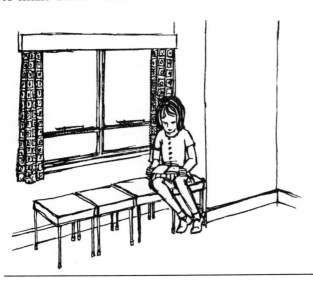

In classrooms where there is a good deal of informal and practical work, it is becoming evident that locker desks, and even dual tables are not really satisfactory.

Tables for four, six or eight children with lino, vinyl or Formica tops, provide a more suitable surface for a great deal of work.

Tables can be made by removing the tops of a pair of old desks or tables and replacing them with a top covered with Formica, lino or vinyl. Old tables with bad surfaces can be surfaced with vinyl.

As schools gradually change to using tables for groups of children, a number of locker desks will become available for other purposes. They can be used in many ways.

A locker desk with the lid removed and replaced with wire netting will make two cages for small animals like mice or hamsters.

If the lids are replaced with plate glass and a light fixed inside, a desk can be used as a tracing table.

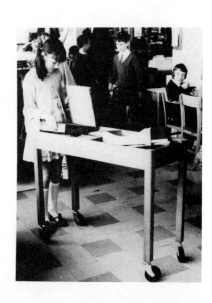

The lids can be sawn up and fitted in again to make dividers so that the desk can be used to display or store books or work cards.

Castors have been added to this desk to make a trolley.

Individual work is encouraged when there are a number of corners where children can retreat to work quietly. These can sometimes be made from existing furniture.

Locker desks can form the basis of a series of booths or carrels for individual work with tape recorders or playback machines. The desks can be pushed against a wall and a piece of blockboard fixed between each pair.

A shelf unit can be made from desk lids.

Desks can also be arranged to make island units with screens round them. These can be used for individual work or for work with audio-visual equipment.

Space can often be gained by increasing or improving storage, so that working space can be used more fully.

It is sometimes possible to increase the space available for work by filling an alcove with a built-in cupboard. Sometimes storage outside the working areas can be increased by building a cupboard into an entrance lobby or part of a cloakroom. A school store or a cleaners store may be made in this way, leaving the working space for learning materials.

Equipment in frequent use is best stored on open shelves where what is available can easily be seen.

Many working spaces in schools have high ceilings. Some equipment not in frequent use can be stored on high shelves.

Many schools find themselves with a motley collection of unattractive cupboards. They can be given some unity if they are painted the same colour.

In some schools space has been gained by removing cupboard doors. Shelves in the cupboards are then made attractive by papering or covering with plastic adhesive.

Tall cupboards can be turned on their sides and doors and shelves removed. New long shelves can be made from the doors, and old shelves can be used between two cupboards.

Trolleys are useful for many purposes and can be pushed away under work benches when not in use.

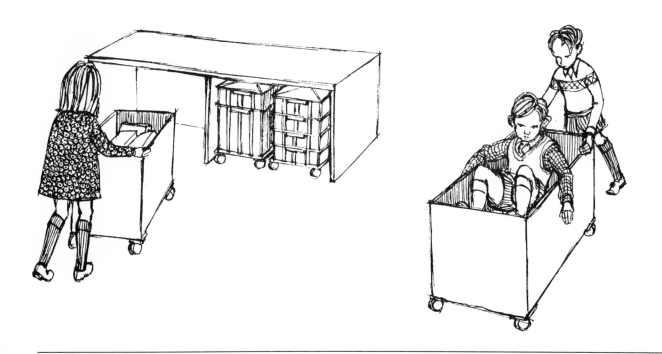

A hanging rail attached to a box trolley converts it into a dressing-up trolley.

The simple box trolley can be used for scrap materials of all kinds and for large play equipment like bricks.

A box trolley can be made from an old table.

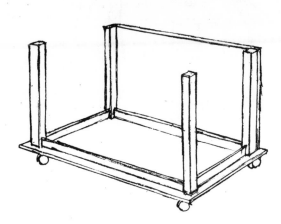

The sides are filled in with blockboard.

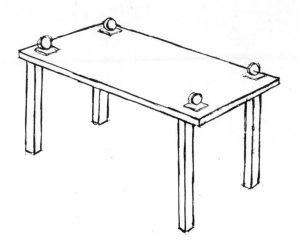

Castors are attached to the table top.

The completed trolley.

Another storage unit made from an old table.

Another useful type of trolley consists of a
series of stacking boxes.

These boxes can be used to store equipment of
various kinds.

A deep plastic box, perhaps with a single
shallow box on top and a lid is excellent for clay
storage.

Needlework is well served by stacking boxes.
Different materials can be kept in the different
boxes and these can be pulled alongside a group
of children for work.

A trolley which can be pushed away under a work top makes a good storage place for paint.

It can be pulled out when it is needed and children can get round it. It is also easier to clean than a cupboard.

A trolley is also valuable for work with sand and water.

A trolley of small boxes can be useful for storing equipment and materials.

Some plastic boxes can be suspended on the wall.   Plastic boxes which stack may be useful.

If tables rather than desks are used, individual storage of children's property will be needed. This can be provided in various ways.

There are a number of drawer units on the market.

It is possible to buy units for plastic trays. One very cheap way of providing these trays is to use seed boxes.

It is often useful to have storage units on castors so that they can be drawn alongside a group of children.

These can also be placed on shelves.

Some of the suggestions given in this booklet involve removing doors. These can be used in various ways. A door may make a useful room divider. This door is held in place by book shelving.

Cupboard doors may be supported by bricks or blocks of wood to give paper storage.

Cupboard doors can be covered with soft board
or expanded polystyrene sheets to provide display
boards. Covered with hardboard and battens,
they can provide extra book display. If they are
hinged to the wall, two surfaces are available
for use.

Doors can also be used to make working
surfaces of various kinds.

Teachers vary a great deal in the degree to which they use a blackboard. Some need more space than they have. Others barely use one. It is worth considering the degree of use the blackboard gets and adding to it or reducing it accordingly.

The teacher who would like more blackboard space may find a hinged board helpful.

The teacher who could do with less may like to cover part of the board with corrugated card, which can be used for display.

Some space should be available for children to write and draw on the board.

The old-fashioned blackboard and easel seems rather dangerous in classrooms where there is a good deal of movement. It is safer to fix boards to the wall, where they take up less space.

Where there is a good deal of group work and where children no longer face in one direction only, boards should be placed on more than one wall, if they are used.

Whiteboard, used with felt pens, has the advantage that colour is being used on a white surface in a similar way to that used by the children in their books. It is also much cleaner in use than chalkboard. Adhesive whiteboard material for converting blackboards to whiteboards is available.

Whatever is done to improve old buildings it is vital to remember that the school environment is setting standards of environment for the children. Financial difficulties will always make it difficult for teachers to provide as much of quality in the environment as they would wish. Nevertheless we should all ask ourselves the following questions at frequent intervals:

1. What is there of real quality in this environment which children will absorb and which will perhaps unconsciously contribute to aesthetic standards?

2. Does this room/work area provide as visually and emotionally satisfying environment as I can achieve with what I have at my disposal?

3. What is there in this environment to stimulate children to learn?

4. What is there in this environment which will give children pleasure?

'We should like to see the schools becoming, much more than most of them now are, places in which the children are surrounded by many examples, old and new, of taste and discrimination— furniture, clocks, fabrics, ceramics, pictures and books. It should be the object of every school to do all in its power to add to the beauty of its equipment and environment, in exactly the same way as a householder with a sensitive eye for beauty will make such constant additions, improvements and adaptations as his means allow to the house and garden in which he lives. In recent years the public have become familiar with the interiors of many great houses which were once closed to all but a privileged few, and which are now worth seeing because their former owners had taste, thought their own surroundings important and took trouble with them. We should like to see schools set out on the same course, so that in time every school in England is worth visiting, not only for what goes on in it, but for the surroundings it gives to its children and the example it sets of civilised living.'

From *Children and their Primary Schools*
H.M.S.O.

LANGUAGE AREAS

One of the major areas of change in primary education is in language work. Our growing understanding of the part that talk plays in children's learning has changed our schools from places where most of the talk was done by the teacher to places where teachers search for ways of starting profitable talk with children. We have come to recognise that if a child is to make language his own, he must use it in context and in talk as well as in writing.

Changes in organisation towards more individual learning have led to a greater use of written language as a medium of individual instruction. A child now may often work from instructions on a work card, where formerly the teacher told him what to do. This means that reading with understanding is even more important than formerly as a medium of other learning. It also means that we need to consider learning to read as a process which goes on after the initial learning, to develop the skills of using books and of reading appropriately in different situations.

Reading is also something we do for pleasure and one of our aims is to lead children to a real enjoyment of books.

Writing too, plays a rather different part. We now tend to see it more as a way of recording experience, and we try to use the motivation that this provides as an opportunity to help children to acquire the skills of using written language.

All these changes bring with them the need for a different use of space, equipment and materials. This book suggests some ways in which some of these needs can be met.

The book areas in a school should attract children to books, so that they come to associate reading with pleasant surroundings.

The ideal book area should be something like an attractive living room in a home with many books.

If possible, book areas should be fixed, so that they can be furnished appropriately. Folding book cases are usually less satisfactory than wall shelving. A good arrangement

is an area with three sides provided with low shelving for books, and the fourth open to other work space.

Books need to be easily available to children. If possible each group of rooms should have its own book collection, with a school collection of the more expensive books available to everyone. The collection which is always nearby makes it easy for the teacher to help children in their use of books.

Sometimes it is possible to find a space which can be shared by a group of classrooms. This can increase the number of books available to the teachers and children concerned. A space of this kind could be made by clearing cloakroom space which is not really needed.

Many corridors can provide a space for books if they are stored on narrow-lipped shelves. If the corridor is wide enough, chairs, stools and even tables can be provided for children to use.

Quite a small alcove in a corridor or classroom can be shelved to provide some space for books.

A cupboard at right angles to the wall can be used to form a book area and shelves can be fixed to its back.

The school entrance hall is often under-used and can make an attractive book area.

Dark corners can be given proper lighting and can be used for books.

Old blackboards or doors can be used to make room dividers, which have shelves each side and can be used for books.

Even a narrow piece of wall can be shelved to provide book display.

A store room which is not really needed might be used as a book area.

A variety of book storage is needed in a book area. It is particularly important to have plenty of shelving which allows the front covers of books to be shown.

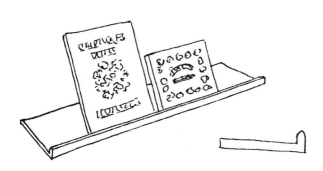

Narrow-lipped shelving may do this. The shelf can be as narrow as three inches, and this is particularly useful where space is limited. Even a strip of hardboard or cardboard pinned or stuck into place along the front edge of a shelf will serve to hold books in place.

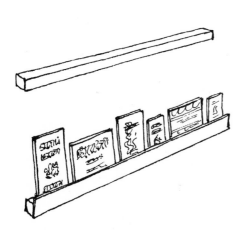

Another useful form of shelving where space is limited is the slot type. Here a one-inch batten is screwed to the wall and then a strip of hardboard two to three inches deep is fixed to the front of it, so that books are held in place.

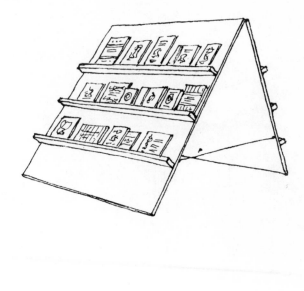

This kind of shelving can be fixed to an old blackboard or other flat board. This can be hung from a wall or propped against it.

If a board of this kind is propped at a sufficient angle the shelf alone will support the books and they will stay in place.

Old folding book cases, which are no longer very satisfactory as free-standing units, can be hung from the wall.

If hardboard strips are fixed along the edges of the shelves of these bookcases, wire will not be needed to hold the books.

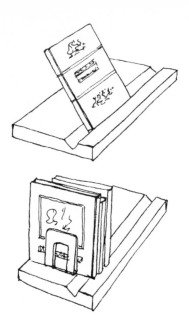

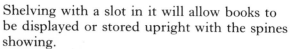

Shelving with a slot in it will allow books to
be displayed or stored upright with the spines
showing.

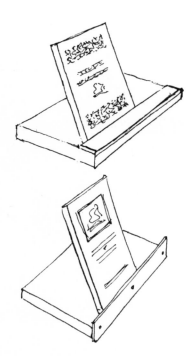

Ordinary shelving can be altered slightly to
make it easier to display books by sticking or
nailing strips of hardboard to the surface of
the shelf along the front edge, or sticking a
strip along the shelf edge.

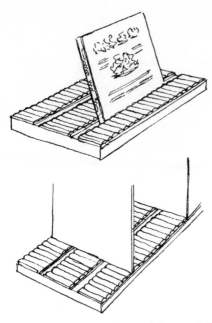

If corrugated hardboard is used for this purpose and fixed to the top and bottom of the shelves, dividers can be slid into place between the two pieces of hardboard when they are needed.

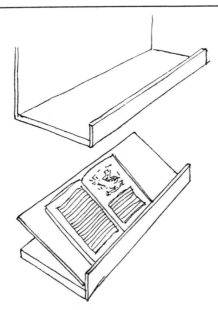

A sloping shelf with a lip at the bottom is useful for book display. It can be provided easily by fixing a strip of wood or hardboard to the edge of an existing shelf, and then propping a piece of wood or hardboard against the lip.

Book shelves can be made very cheaply using broom handles or dowelling, or blockboard and timber.

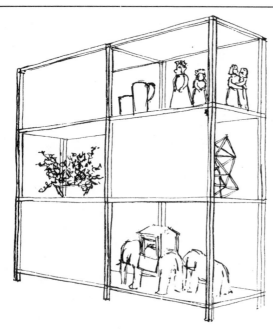

They can also be made from Dexion Speedframe. This kind of shelving unit can double as a room divider.

Many different kinds of shelving are available
in different materials.

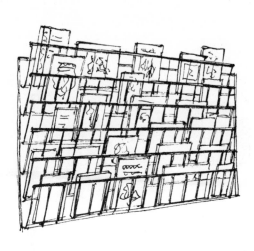

Racks can be hung from the wall, or used as a
free-standing unit.

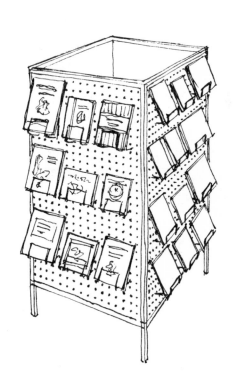

Some book cases and racks can be arranged
to make an island display.

Shelving for books needs to be adjustable.
There are many ways of providing this.

Spur shelving supports can be bought and fixed to the wall.

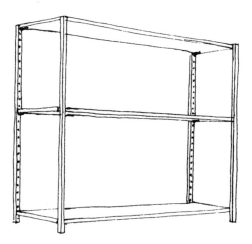

Speedframe is obtainable with slots for shelving.

Shelving units can be hung on the wall.

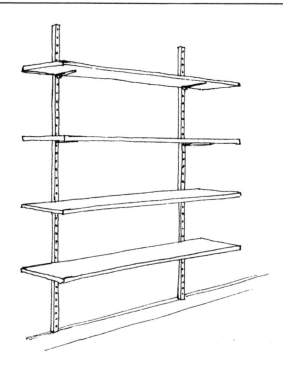

Speedframe can also be fixed to the wall.

Some shelving systems provide for adjustable shelving.

The ladder-type of unit provides excellent shelving but is usually expensive for school use.

These slotted wooden uprights allow for display and adjustable shelving.

Where shelves are to be built holes for pegs can be drilled in the uprights and the shelves placed as necessary.

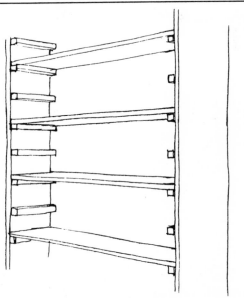

Shelves can be made to rest on battens fixed to the uprights. This allows the shelves to be moved as necessary.

A good deal of shelving can be provided in a small space if hinged panels are used. Battens, with strips of hardboard to retain the books, give a large area for book display.

Book troughs are particularly useful for large books. They can be bought or made from old locker desks.

Books trolleys are useful when books have to be moved from one place to another. There are a number of attractive trolleys on the market.

A trolley for books can be made from Speedframe.

Two boards can be hinged back to back on a framework. Shelving can be fixed to each board and castors added to the base.

Book areas need more than shelving for books.

A work top may be needed. It is useful to have some shelving above it.

Even a narrow shelf can be useful for writing and need take up very little space.

Book areas really need tables if they are to be used for work with books. But if a book area is placed so that table space is available nearby, this may serve. Some new schools have a book area adjacent to dining space, so that additional table space is easily available for most of the day.

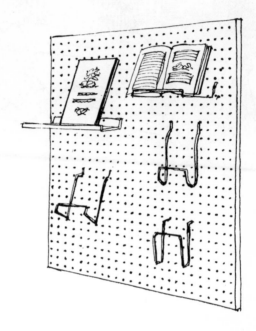

Pinboard is needed in book areas for all kinds of purposes. It may be used to draw children's attention to new or relevant books, or to display their work.

Pegboard is also useful for book display and there are many fittings which can be used for books.

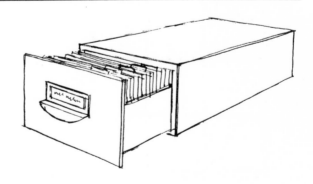

There are several small items of equipment which may be useful in book areas.
Metal book-ends fit under books and hold them in place.

A card index of books may be needed.

It makes a difference if carpet can be provided in a book area. When a school cannot afford to buy a complete piece of carpet, it can be improvised in various ways. Where a complete carpet is used, it is important to fix the carpet edges to the floor, so that they are not kicked up. Special edging is available for this purpose. Carpet not only gives a feeling of quality but also provides a space where children who prefer it can work on the floor.

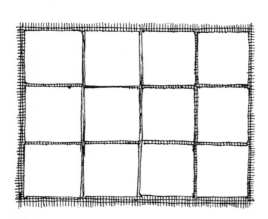

Carpet samples can be stuck onto hessian or on to an old carpet. It is wise to choose pieces which blend well together.

Carpet tiles can be bought and laid. These can be purchased a few at a time as money is available.

If book areas are to give a feeling of quality, it is helpful if the furniture in them can be different from normal school furniture. Ideal provision might include child-sized easy chairs and attractive tables and curtains.

Some schools have managed to acquire a number of old easy chairs. These are much improved if they are given stretch covers.

Even ordinary old school chairs look more attractive when painted and cushioned.

Work cards and reading apparatus pose storage problems, particularly as work becomes more individual. More filing systems are needed in schools.

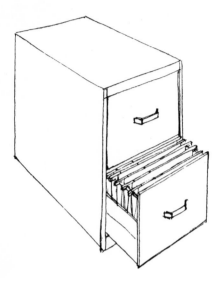

The cheapest kind of filing system is in a filing cabinet which holds hanging files. Two drawer cabinets, which will fit under a work bench, can now be bought in a variety of colours.

Rails for holding hanging files can be fitted into cupboards or can be free standing.

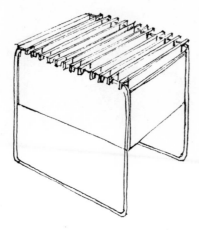 

A variety of free-standing hanging-file systems are available. Some of these are on runners or castors. They can be made with Speedframe. Filing systems of this kind tend to be expensive, but are easy to use. They can be colour-coded in various ways and even quite young children can find material in them.

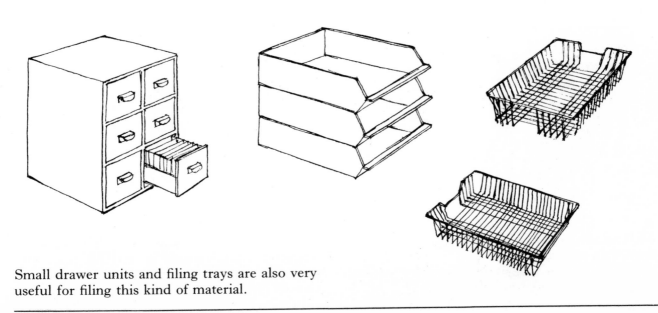

Small drawer units and filing trays are also very useful for filing this kind of material.

Many schools will want to improvise their own
filing systems, because these are cheaper.

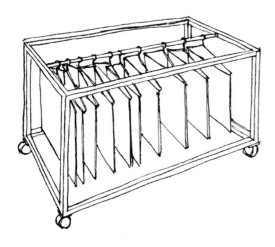

A good way of storing reading equipment and
apparatus is by hanging it in plastic bags on a
framework or a trolley, which could be made
from Speedframe. A trolley can be pushed away
under a bench when not in use.

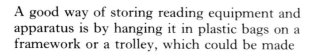

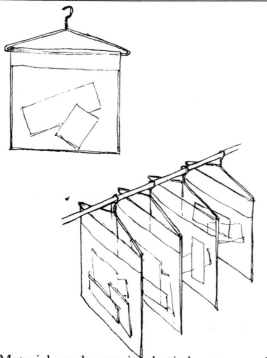

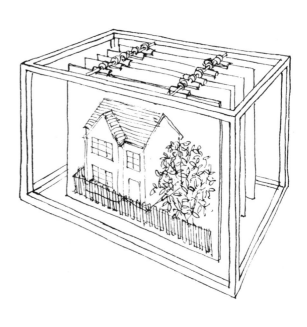

Material can be put in plastic bags suspended
from wire coat hangers.

This kind of system can also be used for charts
and pictures which can be pegged into place with
bulldog clips which have been threaded into
place on rails.

There are also ways of improvising a filing system using existing furniture.

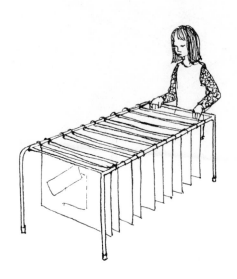

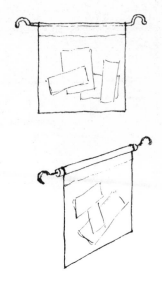

If the top is removed from an old infant table, the frame remaining can serve as a holder for plastic bags, each of which will need a special frame which can be made from wire or by fixing hooks into both ends of a dowel rod.

This kind of filing system also can be hung from a framework on top of a table or work bench, or across an alcove or in a cupboard.

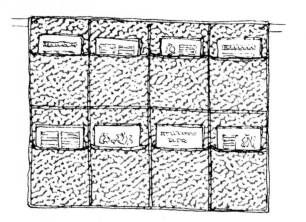

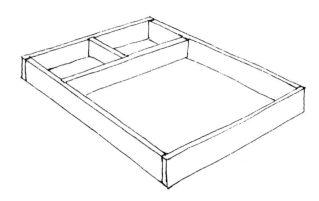

Wall pockets have been used for work card material for many years. Wall pockets can be made from fabric and suspended by eyelets in the corners, or shoe pockets can be used.

Special boxes can easily be made for particular sets of equipment. These can be made from a hardboard base with strips of wood stuck into place to form dividers.

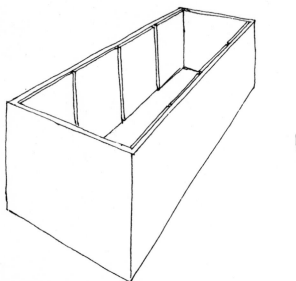

Another way of storing work materials is in long wooden boxes. These can have strips of hardboard stuck to the inner walls of the box, spaced to allow dividing strips of hardboard to be slotted into place when needed.

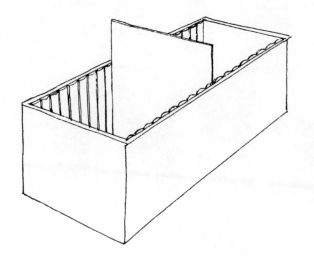

A similar system can be made by lining the walls of the box with corrugated hardboard.

This allows dividers to be slotted in anywhere.

Some reading apparatus is bulky. This is probably best stored in boxes or seed trays on open shelves. Such shelves can be very close together. This means that work tops can be kept clear for work.

Many schools like to store work cards and other reading material in plastic trays.

Various units can be made from broom handles and dowelling, timber or Speedframe.

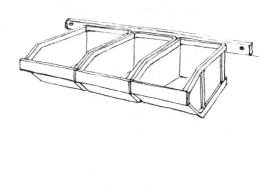

Shelf units without drawers can be useful for storing trays, or stacking boxes with a hand hole can be used. These boxes can also be hung from a special fitment on the wall.

Work cards can be covered with transparent plastic, or varnished with acrylic or sealed into polythene bags. Sealing can be done with a proper heat sealer or by running a lighted match along the opening.

Containers for work cards can be made by cutting away half of the lid of a cardboard box. The remainder of the lid is fixed in place so that the parts are held together. Suitable boxes for this can often be obtained from drapery stores.

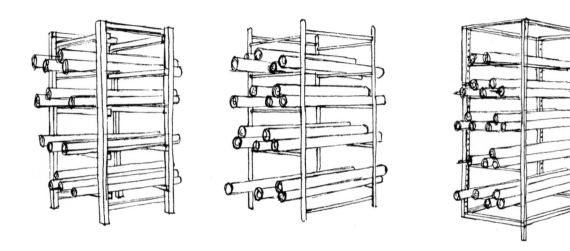

Maps and charts have always posed a storage problem. It is possible to make a useful rack for them using broom handles, timber or Speedframe.

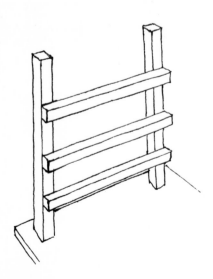

If they are to be kept flat it may be possible to make a simple rack, perhaps using old cupboard doors, blockboard and hardboard.

A rack can be constructed from an old wooden table.

Many schools where storage of work material is limited, could use shelf space more effectively if shelves were divided up more fully.

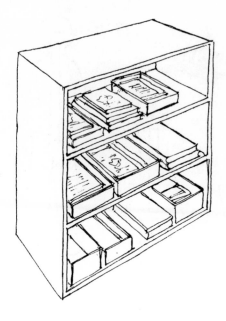

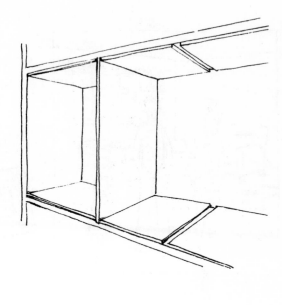

When small items are stored on a shelf there may be a good deal of space above them which is unused.

Use of space on shelves can be increased by inserting dividers. Strips of hardboard need first to be placed at the top and bottom of the shelf to hold the dividers in place. The dividers can be stuck in place with a good adhesive.

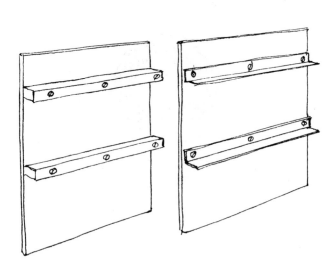

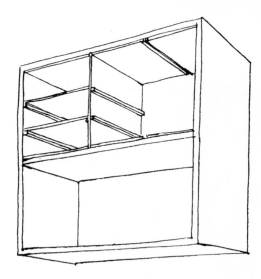

Battens of wood or strips of Dexion angle can be attached to each divider.

These battens can then be used to support hardboard shelves or plastic trays.

Children learning to read need words and pictures displayed in all kinds of ways. In particular they need equipment with which they can build words and sentences.

There are various self-adhesive systems on the market. Flannelgraph and teaselgraph both work because they have material on the back of each item which adheres to background material.

Smooth plastic-film letters and shapes will adhere to other smooth plastic surfaces and to glass. These can be used by the teacher to build up words and sentences with a group of children or they can be used individually. Magnetic board can be used in a similar way.

Individual word- and sentence-building frames
can be made in several ways.

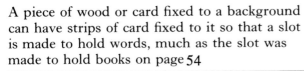

A piece of wood or card fixed to a background
can have strips of card fixed to it so that a slot
is made to hold words, much as the slot was
made to hold books on page 54

Plastic slotting can be stuck to any smooth
surface and allows word building.

Pockets, made from card and preferably fabric
covered, can be stapled onto a background.

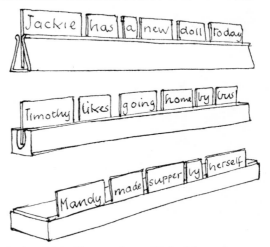

Plastic bookbinding strips will hold cards.
Wood and plastic channelling made for curtain
runners or sliding doors may be used to display
words and sounds.
An upturned box with a lid will hold card
slipped into the side.

Children may be attracted to some language activities by having a special place for them from time to time.

Some schools have found it useful to make a story corner with places to sit, materials and a variety of starting points for story writing available.

Such a corner needs to have a variety of paper and writing tools—perhaps coloured typing papers, coloured inks and felt pens.

It may help to have space immediately available for displaying work written in the story corner, and opportunities for book making.

Handwriting is a skill which needs to be taught and practised. A handwriting corner may stimulate interest.

This should be provided with seating which gives the optimum conditions for writing. There should be pictures and instructions which describe how one should sit.

Children also need pictures showing them how to hold a pen and how to form letters correctly.

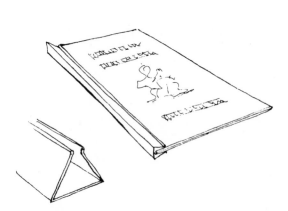

A simple binding of children's work can be made with plastic binding which can be bought cheaply and is slid into place.

The handwriting corner too needs plenty of space for display. There should be examples of really good handwriting from all sources as well as children's own work.

Some individual work may be best done in booths or carrels. There are many ways of providing them.

A screen can be folded round a table or desk.

Or it can be placed on top of a table.

Screens can be fixed between desks or tables, or attached to them.

Purpose-built carrels can also be used.

Screens can provide an exhibition space for a pair of children.

They can also provide a shelf space.

Booths can be made with screens which hinge outward from the wall and peg into place.

The tape recorder offers many opportunities for individual language work. It can be used for children to record their own inventions or it can be used with programmes made by the teacher to help in such work as learning to read. They can also use it to test their own learning of such things as number facts and spelling. A tape may also be used instead of a work card to stimulate work in connection with an exhibition or work kit.

Booths and carrels are invaluable for this, because they allow some isolation.

A child or a group of children can listen to a tape recorder in the corner of a classroom.

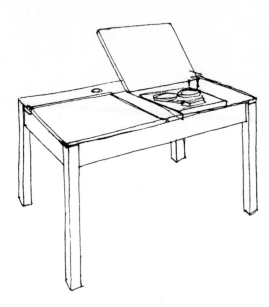

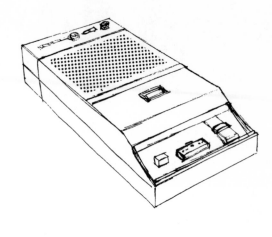

Old locker desks are particularly useful for this work because a tape recorder can be housed inside the locker.

The cassette type of recorder is easier for children to operate than other types.

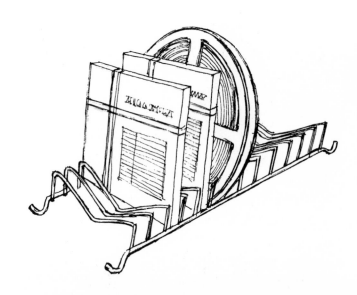

Storage will be needed for tapes. They can be stacked on narrow shelves or stored in a plate rack of suitable size.

Where head sets and junction boxes are available for use with the tape recorder, classroom use is much easier.

Children can then work in a bay or corner without others hearing the programme at all.

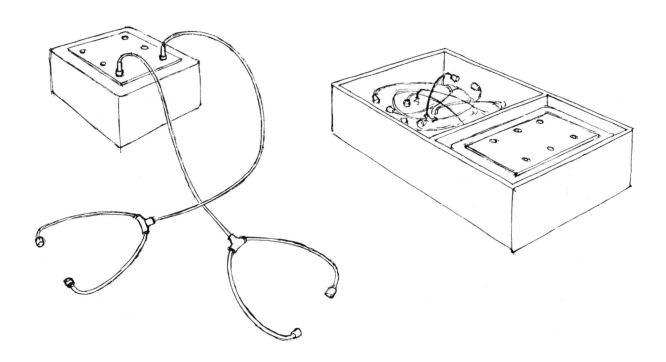

Junction boxes and head sets will need to be carefully stored. It may be worthwhile making a simple box specially for the purpose.

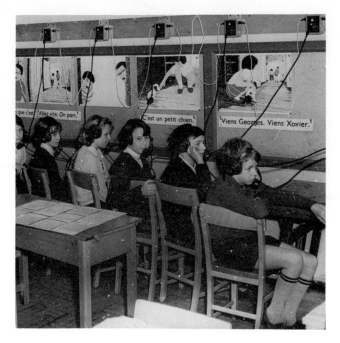

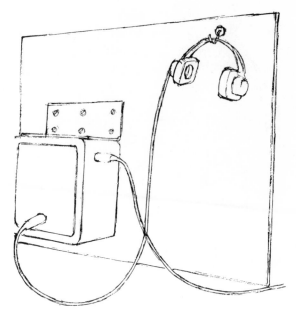

It may be a good idea to have a fixed area for work of this kind, so that the equipment can be hung on the wall after use.

This frame was made from Speedframe and can be moved about the school as it is needed.

The Language Master machine is basically a
tape recorder, but it allows children to pass a
strip of card with a tape on it through the
recorder head and to hear what is written on the
card as they read it.

The machine also allows the child to record on
the tape and to compare his recording with that
made by the teacher. It appears to have many
possibilities, since it allows children to find out
what any word says. Some schools are using it as
a talking dictionary.

Although there are programmes available for use
with it, many teachers prefer to make their own:
blank cards are available. It is also possible to
make one's own by sticking a strip of magnetic
tape to the bottom of a piece of card. Acrylic
appears to be the best kind of adhesive for this
task.

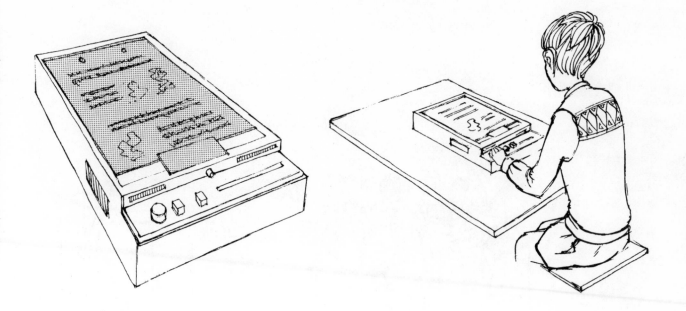

The Synchrofax is a special kind of tape recorder on which a teacher can record a programme on one side of a specially prepared sheet and provide writing to go with it on the other. A perspex cover allows the child using the programme to write also. It can be used with a junction box and head sets.

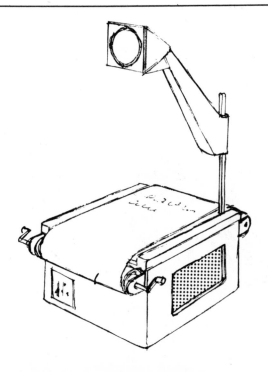

The overhead projector has many uses in school. It has the advantage that material for a group can be prepared and stored after use. Any drawing or printed material in black and white can be copied onto transparencies and projected.

There is a very real place for filmstrips and transparencies which can be projected by the children themselves, perhaps with a tape which tells them what to do.

This can easily be set up in the corner of a classroom; or a storeroom may provide a useful place.

Projection can be on to a piece of plain wall or a sheet of card or paper. A small daylight screen may be useful with groups of children.

Material of this kind may be made up into kits, perhaps including tape, transparencies, work cards, games, pictures and other material. These will need to be well stored and clearly labelled.

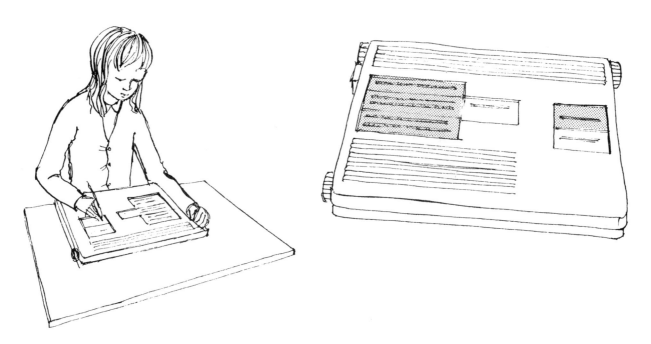

Various small teaching machines can be useful with individually programmed material.

A PLACE TO PAINT

Work with materials is a very important part of the school curriculum but needs more space than many schools can afford to provide.

Many materials require a good deal of clearing up after use, especially if the same space is subsequently to be used for work with books or some other activity requiring clean conditions. This creates many difficulties.

It is easiest to provide well for this work in a programme where only a small group is pursuing a messy activity at any given time, and where an area of the classroom or work space can be given over almost entirely to work of this kind. By varying provision over the course of a term or year, it is possible to provide a variety of work in a comparatively small space, especially if additional space, such as corridor, cloakroom or outside area, can be used.

There should, if possible, be an area where drawing and painting materials are always available and easy to use. Sometimes this area can also provide opportunities for work with scrap materials or collage, or work with plaster or carving. At other times provision might be made for printing on paper or on fabric and fabric dyeing.

Clay is exceptionally messy and really needs a space to itself with easy access to the outside. If provision is shared, it may be possible to find a corner of the building which can be set up for this work.

Work with wood is often noisy and needs a place where the noise will not be too disturbing to others. Sometimes it can be done out of doors.

Clean work with materials, such as weaving, needlework or work with paper, can be done anywhere clean, but needs its own provision of storage.

In this book, the needs of most of the major kinds of materials are considered and suggestions are made about the kind of space, storage and equipment needed. It will not be possible in most schools to provide for them all at the same time.

A good deal of work with materials must be planned in relation to sources of water. It is also important to plan so that there is not too much circulation through work areas. It is worth looking for possible places outside the classroom where some of this work can take place, perhaps on a shared basis, for small groups of children.

Some painting or other work can take place on one side of a corridor or in a cloakroom bay which is not needed for coats.

Outdoor space can be valuable for messy activities like work with clay, and noisy ones like woodwork.

An under-used store room, if it is well lit, may
make a suitable place for cookery or needlework
or any of the cleaner crafts.

Sometimes a landing at the top of a staircase
will give additional space.

All work with materials needs a working surface and it is often difficult to find a large enough surface in school. Additional table-top space may be made by putting a piece of block-board between battens on the backs of two locker desks.

The blockboard may be fixed permanently, or it can be made to drop into place when it is needed.

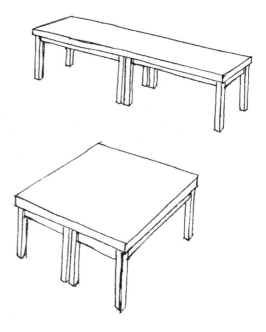

Another way of providing working surfaces which can be removed when not needed is to make a series of covers to go on top of a group of desks. These need a batten round the edge to hold them in place.

Where the insides of desks are not needed or old tables are available, a new top can be made with blockboard, with a Formica or vinyl surface.

Where no permanent provision can be made, it is possible to use a sheet of hardboard or a sheet of very thick card; these can be painted, or a sheet of vinyl can be used.

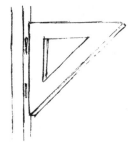

Flaps attached to the wall make further working surfaces when they are needed. They can be

hinged upwards with a display board on the under side.

Children choose to do a good deal of practical work standing up or on the floor. Chairs are not really necessary for much work with materials.

Where seats are needed stools are more useful than chairs, because they can be pushed away under the table when they are not needed.

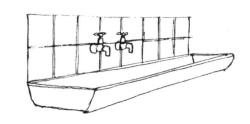

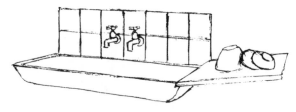

Many of these activities require water. The most satisfactory general-purpose sink is a trough, because it allows several children to use it at once.

Sinks in school need a tiled splash-back. Tiles are easily stuck into place with tile cement. A drainer or an adjacent shelf is essential.

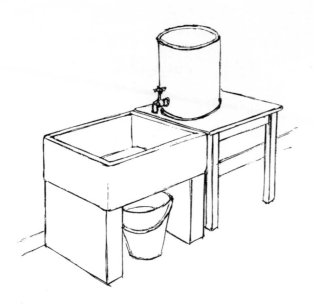

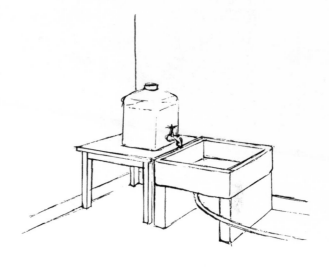

When there is no water supply available, it is possible to improvise by using a container with a tap, such as an old urn or a polythene wine container. This can sometimes be filled with a hose pipe.

Water from these containers can flow into a bowl or bucket, but a sink is preferable, even if waste has to be collected in a bucket beneath it. Waste water can sometimes be piped by hose to a drain.

Areas where messy work takes place need floors which are easy to clean. Vinyl tiling makes a satisfactory floor if water is not left on the surface.

Where a floor has to be protected, a sheet of vinyl which can be rolled up after use may be useful.

Open shelving provides good storage for many materials and pieces of equipment, and has the advantage of being easy to check for tidiness and the return of tools.

Cupboards are often easier to use without doors.

Narrow shelves on a wall can be used for storage of materials or for display.

High shelves are useful for storage of large models and equipment not in frequent use.

Simple shelf units can be made very easily.

Temporary shelving can be made using boards on a folding clothes horse.

Various shelving systems are available. This one depends on slotted pieces of wood as uprights.

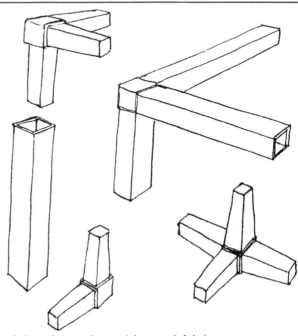

Speedframe can be used to make many different kinds of unit. It is a square metal tube which can

be jointed together with special joints.

Much work with materials involves the storage of small pieces of equipment, such as screws and nails, threads and needles, pencils, scissors, and so on. These need containers which are easy to use and easy to store.

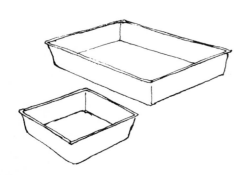

Ordinary seed trays are cheap and give adequate storage.

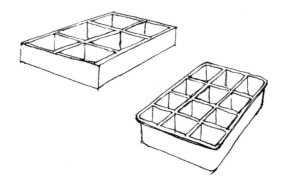

Better quality plastic trays are often larger and can be bought with a variety of divisions in them.

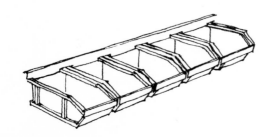

Some plastic trays are stacking. These stack leaving a hand hole. They can also be hung from a special wall strip.

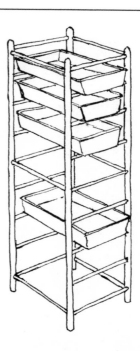

A rack for holding plastic trays can be made very cheaply from four broom handles, joined with dowelling.

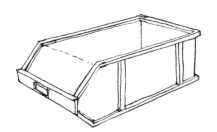

These boxes can also be bought with a clear plastic lid.

They can be made up into a trolley from which boxes can be removed if necessary.

Other boxes are obtainable which stack on top of each other. They come in various depths. A lid can be fitted on the top box.

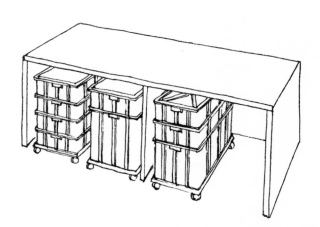

They can be obtained on a trolley with a deep box, useful for clay, or with shallow boxes for needlework materials.

These trolleys can be pushed away under a work top when they are not needed.

Various kinds of units on castors are on the
market and can be used for work with materials.

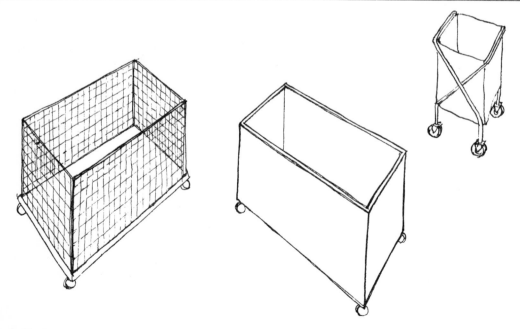

Boxes of all sizes on castors are valuable for
storing materials such as pieces of wood,
cardboard boxes, cartons and other scrap

materials. It is useful to be able to store
material of this kind in types.

Scrap materials can also be stored in a series of cardboard cartons, which should be carefully labelled and placed so that the space about them is clear and can be reached easily.

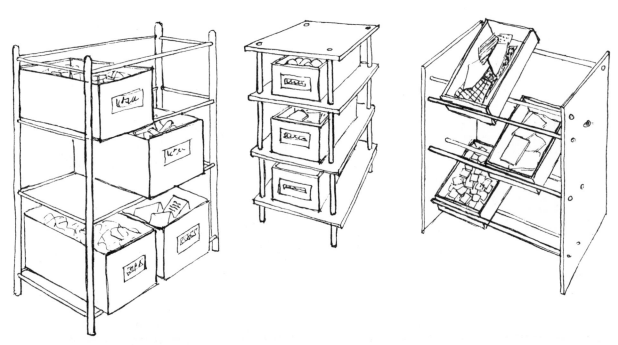

A variety of racks for storing scrap materials can be made from broom handles and dowelling.

Pegboard can be very useful as a place for
storing tools and awkward-shaped equipment.
Many special clips are available.

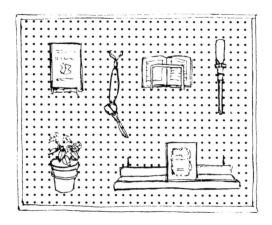 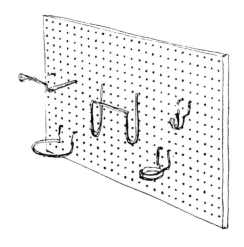

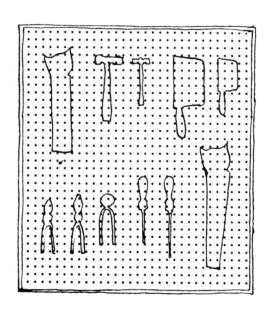

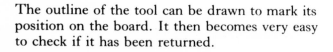

The outline of the tool can be drawn to mark its
position on the board. It then becomes very easy
to check if it has been returned.

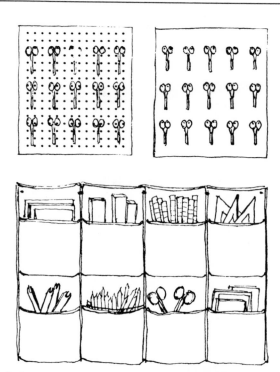

Scissors can be hung from pegboard or a scissor
storage board can be made. Plastic shoe pockets
can be used for small tools and pieces of
equipment.

Much work with materials is messy and it is important to provide adequate covering for children's clothing.

An old shirt worn back to front makes a useful overall.

Another kind of overall which can be bought or made very cheaply.

Aprons can be cut from heavy polythene or plastic sheeting.

Old plastic macintoshes may be cut up to make various kinds of overalls.

Work with materials requires a good deal of space for display. Where pinboard is not available display surfaces can be improvised in various ways.

Corrugated card can be attached to a wall or can be free standing, or it can be made into island units.

Sheet polystyrene and polystyrene tiles are easy to use as display board and can be attached to the wall with special adhesives. Work is then fixed to them with sewing pins. Polystyrene can be bought with a hessian surface. It is also possible to buy hessian-surfaced wallpaper which will take pins.

Much work requires three dimensional display.

This can be on open shelving of various kinds or
on island units or work top.

Displays need to be looked at at various levels.
It is useful to have a number of covered boxes
to use in displays.

A number of the display units on the market
provide for display at different levels. Some can
be pegged together to make different units.

If everything has a labelled place, it becomes easy to return and check tools and materials.

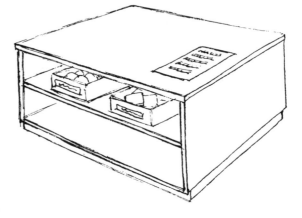

The Dymo labeller makes adhesive waterproof labels.

Lists of the materials and equipment which should be in each place can be stuck to a shelf or door and covered with transparent plastic.

If each shelf has its own list of what belongs on it, and each child is responsible for checking it against a list and tidying a very small part of the room, tidying up becomes quick and easy.

Cleaning up is an important aspect of work with materials which needs to be provided for.

Each room or work space needs certain equipment available.

A broom

A dustpan and brush

A number of dusters, dishcloths and J-cloths.

A mop and bucket

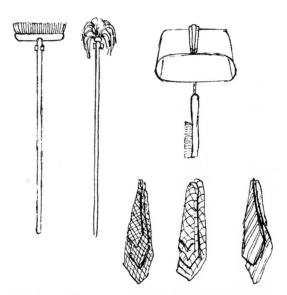

These can be hung on pegboard or on special hooks on the wall.

Each aspect of work with materials has its own particular requirements for space and storage.

Painting and work like collage and junk modelling need a space where children can make a mess without setting undue problems for the cleaner. This work requires easy access to water, a floor covering which is easy to clean, and a degree of separation from clean activities such as reading and writing. It should not take place in an area where other children are constantly passing close to those at work. Flat surfaces, such as table or work top or wall board are needed.

Paper and finished work are most easily stored in a shelf unit. This may provide an additional work top.

Or it can be stored in a cupboard with suitable shelves.

Storage units for paper can be improvised from boards or old cupboard doors. These can be propped apart with blocks of wood.

When quantities of different papers have to be stored on the same shelf, it is easiest to put a few sheets of one kind of paper, and then a few sheets of another and so on, so that no one kind of paper is far from the top of the pile.

A roll of paper for painting can be fixed to the wall and pieces torn off as they are needed.

Paper can be put out for children to use by hanging it from a bulldog clip strung from a clothes line or from the wall.

Easels give ideal surfaces for some but not all types of painting.

A clothes horse with hardboard on each side can be folded round to provide a painting surface for several children.

Hinged boards can be stood on tables for painting. A string will be needed to join the boards at a suitable angle.

A two-sided clothes horse can be covered with hardboard and used as a table easel.

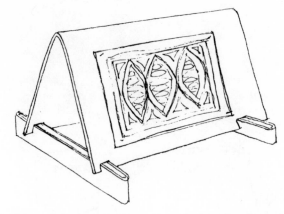

Easels can be made from certain kinds of card, such as Tri-wall.

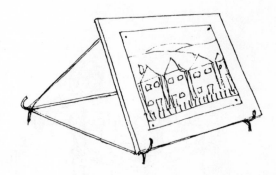

Some wire-frame easels are available.

A board leaned against a wall provides a good surface for painting.

Pinboard can be used in this way also.

A board can be leaned against a wall on top of a bench if there is a ridge to hold it.

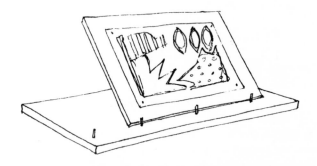

Pegs would also hold it and could be removed when the bench was needed for other purposes.

Paint needs to be stored so that children can get at it easily and so that the area can be cleaned easily.

An ideal form of storage is on a two-tier trolley, which can be pushed away under a work top when not required. This may hold paints, brushes, palettes and water jars.

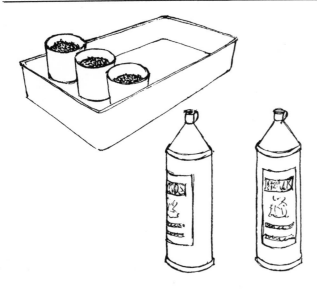

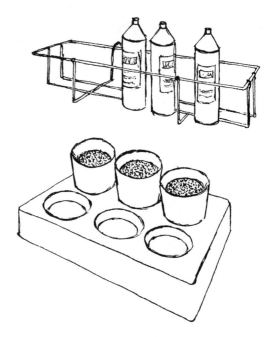

Where a trolley is not available paint containers can be stored in plastic seed trays, which can be easily moved and cleaned.
Liquid soap cartons make good containers for mixed paint.

A number of special racks and stands are now available for storing paint containers.

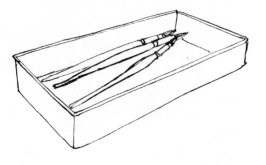
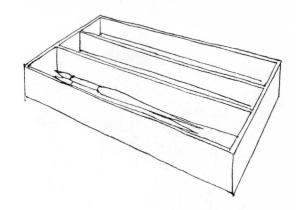

Seed trays can be useful for storing brushes.

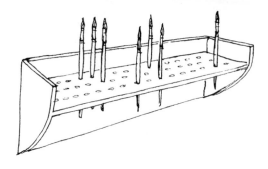

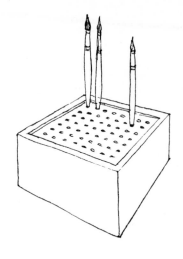

But it is useful to have brush holders, which make it easy to check whether all brushes have been returned. These can be in the form of a wall rack or a block.

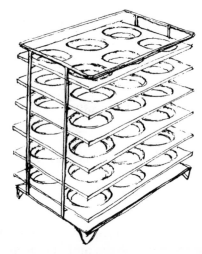

Storage racks for palettes are also available.

Safety water pots may be useful for water or for mixed paint.

Drying work often poses problems.

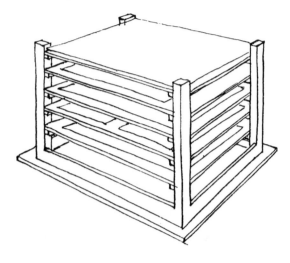

Paintings which are so wet that the paint will run need a special unit which can be built with sheets of hardboard resting on slats fixed on both sides of a box or cupboard framework. These can be placed very close together and the boards can slide out to take the paintings.

A unit of this kind can be made from an old table.

A drying rack for hanging work can be improvised from an old metal frame infant table. The table top is removed and string or wire stretched across the frame. Paintings are then pegged or clipped to the wire.

A ceiling airer is useful for drying work. It can be lowered to the floor for pinning work to it and then hoisted out of the way while it dries.

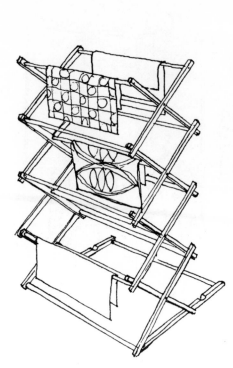

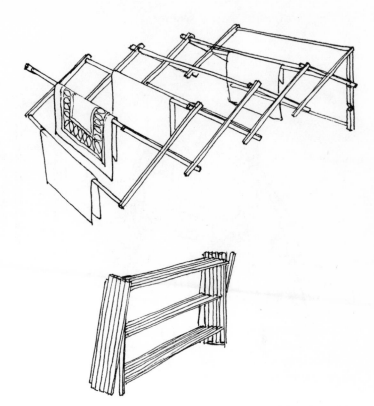

A folding clothes drier can be used for drying paintings. It can be used standing up or suspended from hooks on the wall. It can be folded when not in use.

Even an ordinary clothes line or a clothes horse can serve this purpose. It is also possible to dry paintings by pinning them to a series of moveable arms on a wall.

Work with clay should be separated from other work as far as possible. It really needs an easily washed floor. If there is direct access to the outside, some work can go on out of doors when the weather is fine.

When a wooden floor has to be used a sheet of vinyl can be laid on it.

It is sometimes possible to make a space for work with clay in an under-used cloakroom.

Clay needs adequate storage, so that it can be bought in bulk. Two bins are needed for each colour of clay—one for clay in use, the other for scraps. The scraps bin can be topped up with water periodically so that the clay gets back into working condition.

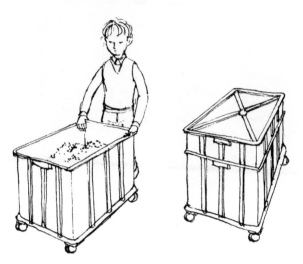

A plastic box trolley can provide good storage for clay and it can be pushed away under a bench when it is not in use. This trolley can be bought with a box to fit on top of the main box, which is useful for storing tools.

Plastic dustbins also make suitable containers for clay.

Clay which is too wet to use can be dried out on a plaster slab.

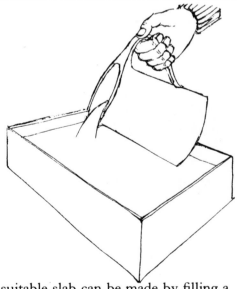

A suitable slab can be made by filling a cardboard box with plaster to a depth of about two inches and stripping the card away when the plaster has set.

A kiln is becoming increasingly necessary if work with clay is to be developed in a school. The most suitable kilns for primary school work are electrically fired. They need more powerful wiring than the usual thirteen amp circuit.

The kiln should be sited so that children do not brush it in passing. A corner is often a good place.

Slatted shelving round a kiln provides a useful space for drying work before it is fired.

Slatted shelving is also useful for storing work in progress, which can be kept damp by wrapping the clay in polythene.

Work with clay requires a surface which is not used for clean activities. Hardboard trays made with the linen side upwards and a one-inch wooden batten round the edge can be placed on tables and will confine the clay.

Alternatively, desk covers like those on page 6 can be used, but with battens on both sides of the cover so that they fit over a group of desks and also confine the clay.

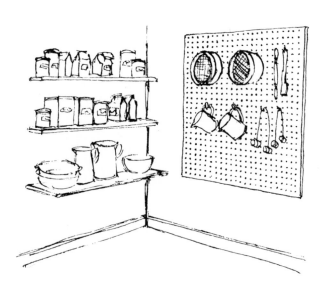

Narrow shelving will be needed for glaze materials, and wider shelves for jugs and bowls for glaze mixing. Pegboard is useful for hanging tools.

Some schools find a table with a well in the centre for clay a useful classroom table for this work.

Needlework needs a really clean working surface, which is large enough for cutting out. A large Formica-topped table is ideal, but where this is not available, it may be possible to use a Formica or vinyl desk cover, placed over several desks.

Bales and large lengths of cloth will need to be stored in a closed cupboard, but much work today is done with small pieces of scrap material. These are stored efficiently in stacking boxes.

Threads, needles and pins, scissors and other small items, can be stored in plastic boxes. The box trolley with lids to the boxes is very useful for this. Sorting trays are also useful.

Sewing machines are best stored so that there is little difficulty in getting them out again. One way of doing this is to store them on a bench under a shelf, so that they can be pulled forward for use.

A long mirror is needed if any dress-making is to be done. This is often usefully placed in a cloakroom where it can have a dual purpose. An ironing board is also needed.

One of the most difficult storage problems in needlework is that of storing children's work. One of the simplest ways to do this is to make a simple rack for boxes.

Fabric printing can take place in a space suitable for painting and may develop out of other work in printing. All forms of printing really need a slightly padded table surface. Newspaper or a blanket can be used for padding.

Printing with dyes will need a washable work top surface. It may be possible to make a table cover from a smooth-surfaced, foam-backed material. This can be stuck to hardboard and placed over a group of tables when it is needed.

Materials for printing and the bowls and jugs needed for dyeing are best stored on open shelves. These can be free standing or they can be underneath a work top.

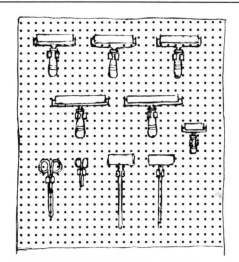

Some equipment, like rollers, can be hung from pegboard.

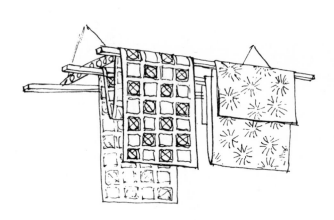

A ceiling airer is the best place for drying materials.

Woodwork areas need to be planned so that noisy work can go on without disturbing other people too much.

The end of a corridor might be suitable.

A cloakroom area may offer a space for woodwork.

It may be possible to use the playground and to do much of this work outside.

Woodwork and some model making needs a really firm wooden table or bench.

Ideally, we would like to have proper benches for this work, but we often have to improvise.

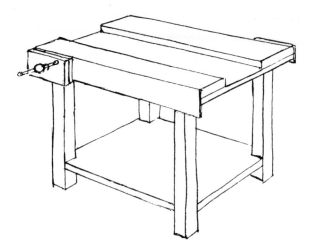

If possible, there should be a vice attached to it.

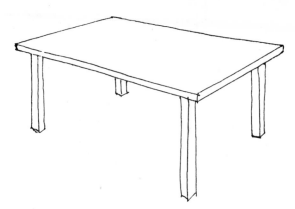

An old kitchen table can be cut down and may serve well.

A workhorse may be a cheaper form of provision for some of the work.

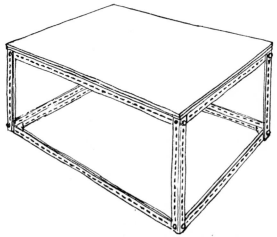

It is possible to make up a work bench from Dexion slotted angle and to make a top from firm board.

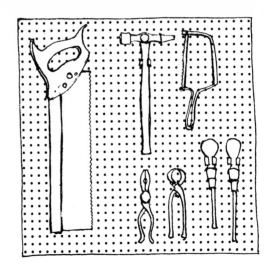

Woodwork tools are best stored on pegboard.

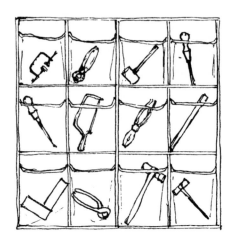

Shoe pockets may be useful for some smaller tools.

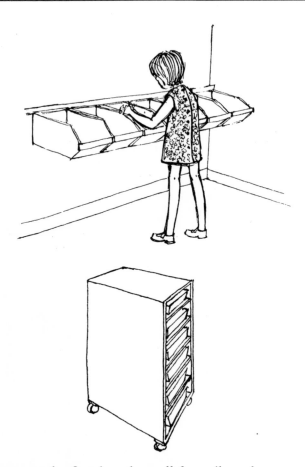

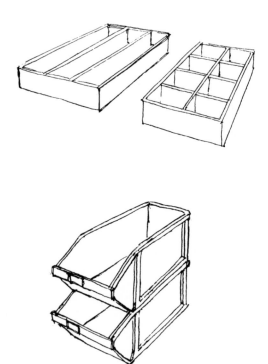

Boxes can be fitted to the wall for nails and screws.

Boxes can be fitted into a trolley.

Sorting trays are also useful for nails and screws.

Stacking plastic boxes can also be used.

Large pieces of wood can be stored on racks. A very simple one can be made from dowelling and broom handles. This will hold the lighter pieces of wood.

Smaller pieces can also be stored behind bars set across a corner or alcove.

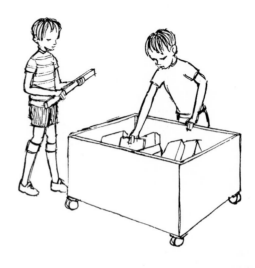

Really small pieces of wood can be sorted into boxes on castors.

Weaving is a fairly clean craft and much of this work can be done in areas also used for reading and writing or needlework.

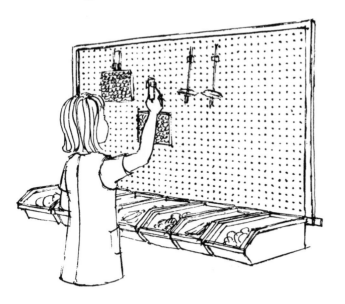

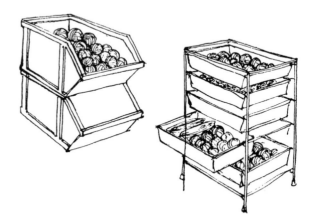

Storage will be needed for such tools as carders, spindles, heddles, and so on. Some of these can be stored on pegboard; others may be better in boxes.

Storage is also needed for yarns. Boxes and trays are useful for this.

Most looms used in primary schools are used on tables and almost any clean and smooth table surface is suitable. Some looms are worked from a hook on the wall.

Looms are generally very difficult to store. Small looms can be hung from pegboard or from hooks on the wall. Larger looms will need shelving.

If this work is to be developed, facilities for cleaning and dyeing wool will be needed. The necessary bowls and dyes are probably best stored on open shelving. Yarns and materials will need to hang to dry. Some form of airer is needed for this.

Cooking is now playing an increasing part in primary school work and in a number of schools children are able to use small cookers.

It is a good idea to try to create a special area for cooking, where a stove can be fitted into a bench run. Small stoves, like the G.E.C. Little

Treasure, can be mounted on a low plinth to bring them up to bench height for children.

The cooking area needs open shelves for ingredients.

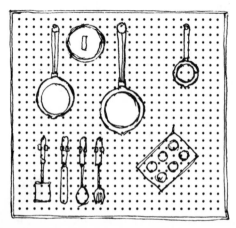

Pegboard is useful for hanging saucepans and other utensils.

A Formica-topped table is needed for children to work at. Pinboard near this provides a good place to pin recipes, which are then kept clean.

If possible, some kind of home area should be near the cooking area so that children can cook and then serve and eat what they have made.

This kind of work leads naturally into the home economics work of the secondary school.